W9-AOL-635

★ SPORTS STARS ★

# NOLAN RYAN
## STRIKEOUT KING

by Howard Reiser

CHILDRENS PRESS ®
CHICAGO

Picture Acknowledgments

Cover, Focus On Sports; 6, AP/Wide World; 9, UPI/Bettmann; 10,12,
Focus On Sports; 13, 16, 19, AP/Wide World; 20, TV Sports Mailbag; 23
(all 3 photos), National Baseball Library, Cooperstown, NY; 24, 26, 27,
28, 29, AP/Wide World; 31, National Baseball Library, Cooperstown, NY;
32, 33, 35, 36, 38, 40, 41, 42, AP/Wide World; 47, National Baseball Library,
Cooperstown, NY

Project Editor: Shari Joffe
Design: Beth Herman Design Associates
Photo Editor: Jan Izzo

Reiser, Howard.
    Nolan Ryan : strikeout king / by Howard Reiser.
        p. cm.–(Sports stars)
    ISBN 0-516-04365-X
    1. Ryan, Nolan, 1947 –Juvenile literature. 2. Baseball
players–United States–Biography–Juvenile literature.
I. Title. II. Series.
GV865.R9R45    1993
796.357'092–dc20
[B]                                          92-35741
                                                CIP
                                                 AC

# NOLAN RYAN

## STRIKEOUT KING

Nolan Ryan may have been the best pitcher ever. He won more than 300 games. He pitched seven no-hitters. He struck out more batters than anyone. He holds dozens of records.

Nolan has thrown the ball faster than any pitcher. Faster than Roger Clemens. Faster than Tom Seaver. Faster than Sandy Koufax. Faster than Bob Gibson.

When in high school, he tried out with the New York Mets. "He was amazing," recalled Casey Stengel, the Mets manager at the time. "He threw so fast, I could not see the ball."

When Nolan pitched, the crowds buzzed with excitement. Fans loved to see Nolan strike people out. They also cheered for him to pitch a no-hitter.

The only ones not happy when Nolan was pitching were the hitters on the other teams. That's because they didn't like to strike out.

Nolan struck out nearly 6,000 batters. He struck out 200 or more batters in a season 15 times. He struck out 300 or more batters in a season 6 times.

"Nolan Ryan threw the ball harder than any pitcher I ever saw," says Hall of Fame catcher Johnny Bench. "He threw the ball a hundred miles an hour. He was awesome."

Nolan Ryan is a kind, considerate person. He speaks softly and is very polite. "My parents taught me to respect others," Nolan says. "They taught me to treat others like I wished to be treated."

In 1993, Nolan completed his fifth year with the Texas Rangers in the American League. It was his 27th year in the major leagues. This gave him the record for the most seasons ever played by a major-league baseball player.

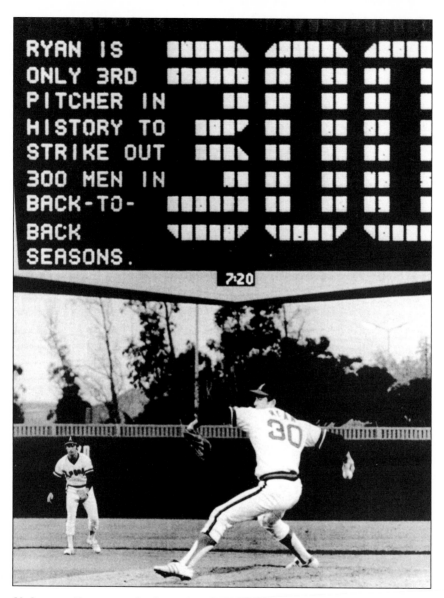

RYAN IS
ONLY 3RD
PITCHER IN
HISTORY TO
STRIKE OUT
300 MEN IN
BACK-TO-
BACK
SEASONS.

7:20

**Nolan on the mound after pitching his 300th strikeout of the 1973 season**

**Nolan lifts weights to remain in top condition.**

"Nolan is an amazing person, an amazing athlete," said New York Yankees star Don Mattingly in 1992. "He works so hard to stay in great shape. That is why he is still one of the hardest throwers in baseball. It is an honor to play against him."

Nolan has always taken care of himself. He lifts weights and does other kinds of exercise to remain in top condition. This helped him to feel strong and to continue to pitch the ball very fast. "It is very important to be in good condition," says Nolan. "If I did not work hard, I would never have been able to pitch this long."

Nolan Ryan was born in Refugio, Texas, on January 31, 1947. His first name is really Lynn and his middle name is Nolan. But his parents began calling their son by his middle name when he was very young. He has been called Nolan ever since.

**Nolan relaxing at home in Alvin, Texas**

Nolan was the youngest of six children.
He had four sisters and one brother. Nolan's
father, Lynn, Sr., and his mother, Martha,
moved their family to Alvin, Texas, when
Nolan was six weeks old.

"I always loved Alvin, and its wide open
spaces," says Nolan. "I loved the farm animals,
the fishing, and the friendly people. I have
played in different cities across the country.
But my roots are in Alvin. I still live there."

**When not playing baseball, Nolan enjoys working on his farm.**

He began playing little-league baseball when he was eight years old. Nolan loved baseball so much, he even wore his baseball cap to school. Nolan's family often watched him play ball. Even his dog, Suzy, watched Nolan play. When Nolan hit a home run, Suzy would bark happily.

Nolan made the little-league all-star team when he was 11 years old, and again when he was 12. When not pitching, he played other positions. Nolan was very good. But, he insists, "I was not the best player."

Nolan attended Alvin High School. He began pitching very hard when he was in his second year. Even at that time, Nolan could throw as fast as some major-league pitchers. But he was as proud of his basketball ability as he was of his fastball.

"I was the center on the basketball team," recalls Nolan. "I had grown to 6 feet 2. I could jump. Our team had a record of 27 and 4 in each of my last two years. I was planning to play basketball in college."

Nolan was a very good basketball player. But it was his fastball that drew raves. In his senior year at Alvin, Nolan won 20 games, lost only 4, and pitched a no-hitter in the state championships.

John "Red" Murff, a scout for the New York Mets, had seen Nolan pitch. Murff believed that Nolan could be a future star. The Mets drafted Nolan in the tenth round of the baseball draft. He signed with the Mets on June 26, 1965.

The Mets assigned him to their rookie-league team in Marion, Virginia. Nolan was 18 years old. After arriving in Marion, Nolan felt lonely. He missed his family. Still, he pitched well. He struck out 115 batters in only 78 innings. The Mets loved his fastball.

Nolan pitched most of 1966 in Class-A ball in Greenville, South Carolina. He won 17 games, lost only 2, and struck out 272 batters in 183 innings. But Nolan was angry that he had walked 127 batters.

The Mets, however, were not concerned. Nolan could throw a pitch faster than anyone, even the great Sandy Koufax. Later that summer, Nolan was promoted to AA ball in Williamsport, Pennsylvania.

"I was now becoming more confident," recalls Nolan. "And I was not as lonely as I had been in Marion, Virginia."

Nolan pitched three games in Williamsport. In his final start, he was supposed to pitch four innings. He was then supposed to catch a plane and join the Mets in New York. At the end of four innings, Nolan had a no-hitter.

Bill Virdon, Williamsport manager, approached
Nolan in the dugout. "Would you like to keep
pitching and try for the no-hitter?" Virdon
asked Nolan.

"Pitching a no-hitter would be a great thrill,"
answered Nolan, "But the thrill of pitching for
the New York Mets is even greater. I would
prefer to leave now."

Virdon looked Nolan straight in the eye.
He shook his hand. "I understand, Nolan,"
Virdon replied. "Go get 'em."

Nolan pitched his first game for the Mets
on September 11, 1966. He faced the Atlanta
Braves. Nolan was so scared he nearly
threw up.

In 1968, Nolan set a Mets club record by striking out
14 batters in one game.

The Braves had Hank Aaron, Eddie Matthews, Joe Torre, and other stars. "It was frightening," remembers Nolan. "Torre belted a home run off me. Later, Aaron said I had one of the best fastballs he had seen."

Former Mets shortstop great Bud Harrelson recalls that Nolan was a "tall, skinny kid" when he first joined the Mets.

"He could really throw hard," remembers Harrelson, who now scouts for the Mets. "And then I saw him throw a couple of great curve balls. I said, 'Wow, he is really something.'"

Nolan did not pitch for the Mets in 1967. He spent six months in the army. The Mets then sent him down to Jacksonville in the International League.

Former Mets pitcher Larry Bearnarth was a teammate of Nolan's that season. Bearnarth will never forget a game Nolan pitched against Buffalo.

"Nolan struck out the first eight batters he faced," recalls Bearnarth. Nobody touched the ball. No fouls, no ticks, nothing. Then Steve Demeter fouled a pitch and the Buffalo fans stood up and gave Demeter a big ovation. We were laughing like crazy on the bench."

No one was laughing a few days later when Nolan hurt his arm while warming up. As time passed, Nolan worried that he would never pitch again.

**Larry Bearnarth**

**Bud Harrelson**

**Nolan in the Mets locker room with some of his teammates**

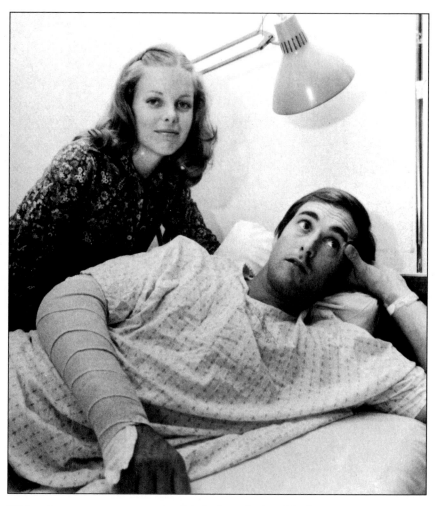

Nolan has overcome several injuries during his long career. In 1975, he had to have surgery on his elbow.

His wife, Ruth, boosted his spirits. He and Ruth had been married that June. Ruth told Nolan his arm would get better. She said he would soon fire the ball again.

Nolan's arm improved that winter in the Mets instructional league. In the spring of 1968, he pitched well. But during the season, Nolan often pitched wildly. He finished the season with six wins and nine losses.

Nolan pitched four full seasons for the Mets. His overall record was 29 wins and 38 losses. He was sad that he had not pitched as well as he would have liked to. But he smiles broadly when he recalls his great performance against the Braves in the 1969 playoffs.

**Nolan in New York City**

**Nolan reacts to winning the pennant in 1969.**

Nolan pitched seven relief innings in the third game. He struck out seven, walked only two, and was the winning pitcher as the Mets won their first pennant. All New York cheered loudly.

But Nolan and Ruth never became used to the fast pace of New York City. They preferred living in a quieter place during the season. Nolan also wanted to pitch more often than he had been pitching with the Mets.

At the end of the 1971 season, Nolan told Ruth that he expected to be traded. One day, the telephone rang in their home. The Mets were calling. Nolan was told that he and three other players had been traded to the California Angels for Jim Fregosi. It was probably the worst trade the Mets ever made.

But it was a great trade for Nolan.

**Nolan and his wife, Ruth**

"At the very start, I was made to feel important," recalls Nolan. "This gave me confidence. It helped establish me as a pitcher." Hall of Famer Tom Seaver, a Mets teammate of Nolan's, says, "Nolie had to pitch a lot. He wasn't getting it with us. With the Angels, he started every fourth day—not every sixth or seventh day."

Nolan pitched eight years for the Angels. During this time, he led the American League in strikeouts seven seasons, struck out more than 300 batters in a season five times, and pitched four no-hitters.

Nolan pitched his first no-hitter on May 15, 1973, against the Kansas City Royals. He pitched his second no-hitter two months later, against the Detroit Tigers. And he struck out 383 batters for the season, breaking Sandy Koufax's record by one strikeout.

In 1973, Nolan broke the all-time major-league record for most strikeouts in a single season.

Jeff Torborg was the Angels catcher when
Nolan pitched his first no-hitter against the
Royals. Torborg recalls, "Amos Otis made the
last out. He hit a ball that I thought would
be a home run. But Ken Barry made a great
catch. It was a thrill to catch this no-hitter.
It was always a thrill to catch Nolan."

**Nolan is congratulated after winning his second no-hitter.**

The 1979 season was Nolan's last with the Angels. It was a hard year for Nolan, even though he again led the league in strikeouts.

Nolan's seven-year-old son, Reid, was struck by a car and badly hurt. Nolan spent a lot of time at Reid's bedside. "It was difficult to concentrate on pitching," Nolan recalls.

**Nolan and his son, Reid, in 1973**

When the season ended, Nolan thought that
the Angels would not offer him a fair contract.
He chose instead to sign with the Houston
Astros in the National League. Nolan would
be paid $1 million a year, the highest baseball
salary ever.

In 1980, his first season with Houston,
Nolan's record was 11 wins and 10 losses.
On July 4, he got his 3,000th career strikeout.
He went on to strike out 200 batters that season.

Nolan pitched nine years for Houston.
He won two strikeout titles, twice led the league
in earned run average, and pitched his fifth
no-hitter, against the Los Angeles Dodgers.
No one had ever pitched five no-hitters before.
"Everyone congratulated me, even former
president Richard Nixon," Nolan remembers.

Nolan waves to the crowd after his 4,000th career strikeout.

Nolan left the Astros after the 1988 season. He led the league in strikeouts that season for the second straight year. Yet the Astros wanted to pay Nolan less money in 1989 than what he had been earning.

Nolan was not happy with that arrangement. Instead, he decided to sign with the Texas Rangers in the American League. "I was very happy to continue playing in Texas," Nolan says.

Both Nolan and the Rangers were happy with each other. In his first three years with the Rangers, Nolan won 41 games and lost only 25. He also pitched his sixth and seventh no-hitters,and led the league twice in strikeouts.

In 1992, Nolan's record was 5 wins and 9 losses. However, he should have had a winning record from the way he pitched. His earned run average for the season was a very respectable 3.72. Often, Rangers pitchers had failed to protect leads that Nolan left them when he was relieved late in games.

Even at the age of 45, Nolan could still throw hard. He was still a great strikeout pitcher. In 1992, he struck out 157 batters in $157 \frac{1}{3}$ innings. "I told Nolan I was amazed he could still throw so hard," relates Harrelson, Nolan's former teammate. "He answered, 'Me, too.'"

**Nolan pitching the 5,000th strikeout of his career**

In 1992, Rangers manager Toby Harrah said that Nolan "is still a great pitcher. He is still as good as any pitcher in baseball. I want him back as a starting pitcher in 1993."

Harrah also praises Nolan as a role model for children. "Nolan is a true hero. I would like my son, Thomas, to grow up to be the type of person that Nolan is," says Harrah.

At the end of the 1992 season, Nolan held
a press conference to announce that he would
return to pitch for a record-breaking 27th season
in 1993. When the season began, however, Ryan
indicated that it would be his last.

It turned out to be a difficult season for Nolan.
Injuries put him on the disabled list several
times, but he kept coming back. Then, while
pitching in Seattle on September 22—two weeks
before he was scheduled to pitch his farewell

**Nolan is mobbed after pitching his sixth no-hitter.**

Nolan meets with his son Reid, pitcher for the University of Texas Longhorns, prior to their exhibition matchup in 1991.

game at home—he felt his elbow "pop." Nolan Ryan walked off the mound, and doffed his cap for the final time. His final pitch was clocked at 94 mph, a speed some pitchers never attain.

Nolan Ryan redefined power pitching. He finished his incredible career with a record 5,714 strikeouts, 11 strikeout titles, 7 no-hitters, 12 one-hitters, 324 victories, and 53 major-league records.

Once, when asked what he would do when he retired, Nolan replied that he would spend more time traveling with his wife and children. "Just because your baseball career is over, it does not mean your life is over," said Nolan. He then offered this advice to young people: "Always do your best, and have fun doing it."

# Chronology

**1947 –** Lynn Nolan Ryan, Jr., is born in Refugio, Texas, on January 31, the son of Lynn and Martha Ryan.

**1955 –** Nolan begins playing little-league baseball.

**1958 –** Nolan makes the little-league all-star team. When not pitching, he plays other positions.

**1965 –** In his senior year at Alvin High School in Alvin, Texas, Nolan wins 20 games, loses 4, and pitches a no-hitter in the state championships.
– The New York Mets draft Nolan in the tenth round of the baseball draft. Nolan signs with the Mets on June 26.
– Assigned to the Mets rookie-league team in Marion, Virginia, Nolan strikes out 115 batters in 78 innings.

**1966 –** Nolan wins 17 games, loses 2, strikes out 272 batters, and walks 127 in Class-A ball in Greenville, South Carolina.
– Nolan pitches three games of AA ball in Williamsport. He is then promoted to the Mets.

**1968 –** Nolan pitches his first full season with the Mets, finishing with a record of 6 wins and 9 losses.

**1969 –** Nolan pitches seven great relief innings in the third game of the National League Eastern Division playoffs against the Braves. Nolan is the winning pitcher and the Mets win their first pennant.

**1970** – Nolan pitches a one-hitter and strikes out 15 in his first start, against the Phillies. The 15 strikeouts were a Mets record at the time.

**1971** – Nolan's record is 10 wins and 14 losses. He is unhappy with the Mets.
– Nolan is traded to the California Angels during the off-season.

**1972** – Nolan wins 19 games, loses 16, and strikes out a major-league–leading 329 batters in his first season with California. He becomes baseball's most exciting pitcher.

**1973** – Nolan pitches his first no-hitter on May 15, against the Kansas City Royals. He pitches his second no-hitter exactly two months later against the Detroit Tigers.
– Nolan strikes out 383 batters for the season, breaking Sandy Koufax's record by one strikeout. He wins 21 games.

**1974** – Nolan pitches his third no-hitter on September 28, against the Minnesota Twins, in his final start of the season.
– Nolan strikes out 367 batters for the season, but also walks 202. He wins 22 games.

**1975** – Nolan pitches his fourth no-hitter on June 1, against the Baltimore Orioles. This ties him with Sandy Koufax for the most no-hitters by a single pitcher in baseball history.

**1980 –** Nolan pitches his first season with the Houston Astros. His salary is $1 million a year, the highest ever paid to a major-league baseball player at the time.

**1981 –** On September 26, with a no-hitter against the Los Angeles Dodgers, Nolan becomes the first major leaguer ever to pitch five no-hitters. During the game, he strikes out 11 batters. It is the 135th time he has struck out 10 or more batters in a game.

**1989 –** In his first season with the Texas Rangers, Nolan strikes out Rickey Henderson of the Oakland A's on August 22 for his 5,000th strikeout. Nolan finishes the season with a league-leading 301 strikeouts.

**1990 –** Nolan pitches the sixth no-hitter of his career on June 11, against the Oakland A's. At age 43, he becomes the oldest pitcher to throw a no-hitter.

**1991 –** Nolan pitches his seventh no-hitter on May 1, against the Toronto Blue Jays. He also ties his own team strikeout record of 16.

**1992 –** In September, Nolan announces that he will return in 1993 for a record-breaking 27th season in the major leagues.

**1993 –** Nolan retires at the end of the season. He leaves the game with a record 5,714 strikeouts, 11 strikeout titles, 7 no-hitters, 12 one-hitters, 324 victories, and 53 major-league records in all.

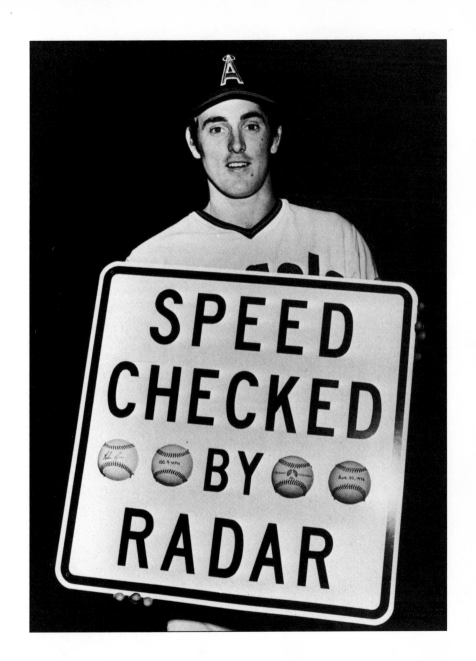

★ ★ ★

## About the Author

Howard Reiser has been a New York City newspaper reporter, columnist, and bureau chief. He has also worked as a labor news writer and editor. Today a political speechwriter, Mr. Reiser covered the major news stories in New York City for more than 25 years.

After Nolan Ryan helped the New York Mets win the 1969 pennant and World Series, Reiser rode atop a flatbed truck, covering the Mets victory parade along Broadway. It was one of the biggest celebrations in New York City's history, as millions cheered Ryan and all the Mets.

Reiser is the author of several other books for young people, including *Jackie Robinson, Baseball Pioneer*. He and his wife, Adrienne, live in New York. They have four children: Philip, Helene, Steven, and Stuart.

# DATE DUE

| | | | |
|---|---|---|---|
| | | | |
| | | | |
| | | | |
| | | | |
| | | | |
| | | | |
| | | | |
| | | | |
| | | | |
| | | | |
| | | | |
| | | | |
| | | | |
| | | | |
| | | | |
| | | | |
| | | | |
| | | | |
| | | | |

#47-0108 Peel Off Pressure Sensitive